Becoming a

Proverbs

PRINCESS

While Waiting for Mr. Right

Sarah White

WESTBOW
PRESS®
A DIVISION OF THOMAS NELSON
& ZONDERVAN

WestBow Press books may be ordered through booksellers or by contacting:

WestBow Press
A Division of Thomas Nelson & Zondervan
1663 Liberty Drive
Bloomington, IN 47403
www.westbowpress.com
1 (866) 928-1240

Because of the dynamic nature of the Internet, any web addresses or links contained in this book may have changed since publication and may no longer be valid. The views expressed in this work are solely those of the author and do not necessarily reflect the views of the publisher, and the publisher hereby disclaims any responsibility for them.

Any people depicted in stock imagery provided by Thinkstock are models, and such images are being used for illustrative purposes only. Certain stock imagery © Thinkstock.

ISBN: 978-1-5127-6876-3 (sc)
ISBN: 978-1-5127-6877-0 (e)

Library of Congress Control Number: 2016920869

Print information available on the last page.

WestBow Press rev. date: 12/28/2016

I would like to say thank you to Halle Hess,
Bethany Lewis, Hannah Hinerman, and Madeline
McLaughlin for their contributions. Without
their stories, this book would not be complete.
I would also like to thank Bethany Storts,
who illustrated the images at the start of each
chapter. I am truly grateful for the kindness
and love that these women show daily.

Dear Heavenly Father,

I come before You today to ask that You be with each and every young woman who reads this book. I pray that Your love, peace, and joy surround her. Open her heart to what You have planned and guide each of her steps. In every moment of her life, I pray that she will turn to You and find her strength in You. I praise You for Your continuous love, and I give thanks for every girl who will receive this book. Thank You for all that You have done and continue to do. Through this book, Your name will be glorified.

With all my heart, I pray in Your Son's holy name. Amen.

TABLE OF CONTENTS

Chapter 1   Becoming a Proverbs Princess 101 1

Chapter 2   Your Knight in Shining Armor 15

Chapter 3   Life While Waiting in Your Tower...... 25

Chapter 4   When Mr. Right Becomes Mr. Wrong .. 35

Chapter 5   Life After the Happily Ever After....... 55

She is clothed in strength and dignity and she laughs without fear of the future. PROVERBS 31:25

Proverbs 31:25 (NLT)

CHAPTER 1

Becoming a Proverbs Princess 101

A woman's heart should be so close to God that
a man should have to chase Him to find her.
—C.S. Lewis

Growing up, I was always the shy, quiet girl. I never imagined that I would turn out to be someone important because the only attention I received came as negative comments made about my appearance and awkward behaviors. I struggled to hold on to any self-worth whatsoever; therefore, I always thought that something was wrong with me. I was

so consumed by who the world was telling me to be that I lost sight of God's perfect plan.

Little did I know that, because of hereditary genes, I tended to experience high anxiety and depression, which hindered me from building confidence. However, after I found that focusing on Christ-driven self-worth and counseling helped me, God showed me what it meant to put my identity in Him. It may have taken me longer than the typical lady to find myself and to discover who I really was, but that's okay because every journey is different. I know I wouldn't change mine for anything. That's why I want to encourage each of you to reflect on your journey and who you are. Now, I can look at myself and see how far I have come. If I had told my middle school or high school self where I am today, I never would have believed it, but thanks to God, He knew my potential better than I ever did!

If you could be any woman in the world, who would you be? Perhaps you might choose Taylor Swift, Selena Gomez, or another famous person. What about a well-known businesswoman or politician? Maybe you chose your mom or a close family member.

Regardless of who you picked, why do you want to be like that person? What makes that woman stand out from everyone else? Now, what if I told you that you were created in the image of someone even greater and given a call to be someone even more special? What if I told you that you were called to be a woman of God? I'm sure many of you have heard this before, but do you know what it really means? You see, it's important to first figure this out and to discover who you truly are before you get into a relationship. Therefore, what does it mean to be the woman God created you to be?

Often, when we think about what a woman of God looks like, we imagine a small, timid woman with her hair in a bun who enjoys knitting and baking in her free time. Although there is nothing wrong with that picture, this woman may look quite different from the one you aspire to be. Nevertheless, when we take a closer look at what scripture actually says, a different picture is painted. In fact, in Proverbs 31 we see that there is a lot more to being a Proverbs Princess than most people realize.

In Proverbs 31, we find that a woman of God is willing to work (vv. 13). She is an entrepreneur who knows how to invest knowledgeably (vv. 16, 18, 24). She is also wise and able to instruct others (vv.

26-27). Furthermore, when it comes to her family, she is the head of her household (vv. 21). Still, even more important than what she does is how she acts. A woman of God is one who not only loves the Lord and her family but also reaches out to the poor and those in need (vv. 11–12, 20, 28, 30). The qualities of a woman of God include trustworthiness, productivity, initiative, compassion, honor, strength, and wisdom, in addition to many more attributes found in Proverbs 31, Titus 2, and throughout the rest of the Bible.

This may seem like a lot to take on, so let's look at some real life examples. One example found in the Bible is Esther. Now, Esther was a beautiful queen, but more than that, she loved the Lord and was willing to risk her life for His people. She was courageous, wise, and pure. Another example is Ruth. When tragedy struck in her life, Ruth's honorable character shined through. She showed true love by following her mother-in-law to a foreign land where Ruth worked to provide for both of them. A more recent example is Mother Teresa, who is known for her charitable works. Years after becoming a nun, she left the convent and dedicated the rest of her life to living with the poor while serving them.

Did you notice how, throughout the examples and

description of a Proverbs Princess, her character was never dependent on the status of her relationship with a man? That's because whether a woman is single or married, she is still able to be a woman of God. Now, imagine if you began to apply this concept to your life, what would change? How would your friends and classmates react if you started acting in a way that reflected God's love? For a moment, let's just imagine that you decide to start living in a manner worthy of your calling. With that choice, you begin to become intentional in your relationships by investing your time in building others up. You then step outside of your close group of friends to include others whom everyone else has seemed to overlook. Similarly, when someone puts you down or makes fun of you, you are able to look past her actions to see a person in desperate need of God's love. Therefore, when people begin to point out the flaws of others and make fun of them, you don't join in. In terms of how you treat yourself, you finally stop defining your beauty by the reflection you see in the mirror, and your intelligence is no longer dependent on the grade at the top of a test. Instead, it's defined by your ability to apply your knowledge in a way that improves the world around you. In every moment, your character and reputation don't resemble a perfect person; instead, you reflect the image of a person who is openly flawed yet always honest, trustworthy, humble, and loving. Basically, you choose to live in a way that causes others to wonder what makes you so different and selfless.

Wouldn't you agree that there's a lot more to becoming the woman God designed you to be than you originally believed?

Dear You,

As you journey through middle school and high school, I encourage you to seek a mentor or spiritual leader who will guide you through this chapter of your life. Look to trusted women in the church and be willing to open up to them. Don't be afraid of people and building relationships. In fact, God actually created us to be relational.

When I was your age, I wish that I would have known the importance of being myself and not trying to be someone else. That's why I urge you to work on bettering yourself instead of copying other people. During this time, please be focused on the important things, rather than boys or your appearance. Trust in those who support you and who keep you accountable. Never forget that this is a time of growing and changing; therefore, use each moment wisely as you work to become more like Christ.

Even though I wouldn't change anything about my story, I still wish someone would have shown me that the important things in life are to love others and to build a relationship with God. That's why I am striving now to build up ladies like you. I hope to guide them to grow in Christ while they find out who they are. I pray that, through my story, you see the importance of growing closer to God as you become the woman He wants you to be.

Love,

Halle

The end of each chapter offers an area for reflection. As you are answering each of the questions, I ask that you take your time. Think your answer through and be honest with yourself. Therefore, later, down the road when you begin to date and are surrounded by emotions and feelings of love, you will have this book as a reminder of what you were thinking at this very moment and what you were learning about having a godly relationship.

What are your outstanding qualities? How can you use these qualities to serve God?

How are you called to be different from the young woman the world is telling you to be? What would change if you started living out your calling from God?

What steps are you going to begin taking now to become more like a Proverbs Princess?

Dear Heavenly Father,

Thank You for creating me in Your image and with a great purpose in mind. As I strive to become the Proverbs Princess whom I am meant to be, I pray that You help me not to lose sight of Your vision. Give me the courage to stand up for what I know is right. Every day, fill me up with Your love so that I can pour it out on everyone I meet. Help me to have the wisdom to make the right choices that will glorify Your name. All in all, I pray that my love for You will be renewed each and every day so that I can only grow closer and closer to You. In Your holy name, I pray. Amen.

Romans 12:2a (NIV)

CHAPTER 2

Your Knight in Shining Armor

The greatest thing a man can do for a woman
is lead her closer to God than himself.
—Anonymous

I'm in my junior year of college, and I've learned a lot about relationships and myself throughout the past few years (although I am far from having it all figured out). In high school, I never really dated. You see, every time I started "talking" to a guy, I would end things before they ever actually began. There always seemed to be something missing. I used to

think that it was because the guys I talked to weren't like the guys in the movies or love songs. However, in all reality, it had very little to do with who the guy was and a lot to do with who I was and my view of relationships. It may sound conceited and even a little silly, but I unknowingly wanted to date myself. Now let me explain before you judge. I didn't actually want to date myself, but I wanted to be with someone who was JUST like me. I wanted him to express love the same ways I did and say what I thought he should say when I thought he should. I wanted someone who knew my every thought and understood me completely. But by wanting someone who was a mirror image of myself, I accidentally put every guy I talked to in a box that limited them.

As I got into a serious relationship with a man of God I truly love, I started to do the same thing. Unfortunately, by doing this, I kept him from being who God created him to be. Simply put, I was being selfish. I wasn't able to see the ways that he showed me love, like always asking me about my day or buying me food when I was stressed. I wasn't able to see his passion for helping others and wasn't willing to accept that he couldn't spend every moment with me. My anger wasn't rooted out of his shortcomings but by my expectations for another to be just like me. Now in my relationship with him, I'm choosing to enjoy the little differences that make him unique. I'm rejoicing in his loves and passions, and I strive to encourage him. Overall, I am learning to be thankful for our differences because they stretch and challenge me to become a better person daily. Therefore, whether you are in a relationship now or in the future, remember that he is first a man of God and then he is your man.

Fairytales and movies portray Mr. Right as a guy with perfect hair, dreamy eyes, and a great smile, who is not only physically fit but flawless in every way. It seems that his only job is to make you happy. However, contrary to popular belief, your Mr. Right is actually called to more than simply buying you flowers and texting you good morning every day. In fact, he is called to be a man of God, but what does that look like lived out?

In Ephesians 5, Paul beautifully described how a godly man should act in a relationship. He explained how a Christian marriage was designed to be an earthly image of the relationship between Christ and His Bride, the Church, for the whole world to see (vv. 23-25). Just as Christ showed love to the Church, your Mr. Right is responsible for showing you love every day; in fact, he is called to love you as much as he loves himself (vv. 25, 28, 33). The type of love I'm talking about here isn't the kind shown in movies or associated with physical attraction. It's the kind of self-sacrificial love that daily puts another above personal desires, comforts, and pursuits. You see, your Mr. Right won't be the type of guy who uses you to meet his needs, while ignoring yours. Similarly, he won't be the one who puts his dreams above yours and always demands his way. If you are wondering whether or not he reflects love and Christ, ask yourself, "Do his actions build me up and strengthen my relationship with God?" For example, he should treat you the way you would want a guy to treat your best friend or someday treat your future daughter.

Despite what you may think, your Mr. Right isn't going to act like the typical guy you meet. He isn't going to be the manly man who is arrogant, rude, and seems to have everything figured out. Those qualities reflect immaturity and lack of Christ. A man of God should reflect love, courage, strength, and leadership. Likewise, your Mr. Right should be willing to admit mistakes, listen, and take advice from others. He should be a spiritual leader, meaning he will lead you closer to God.

Nevertheless, characteristics vary in what each girl believes her Mr. Right should have. One may want her future husband to like to travel and go on adventures while another may want someone who enjoys a good book and cooking together. In all honesty, although these qualities are important, it is first necessary to look at how he reflects Christ. I want you to take some time and write out on the next page what qualities you would like your Mr. Right to have, things such as being willing to serve and having a solid faith or always being friendly to others and inspiring you to become a woman of God. Perhaps, you may write down how you want him to be a great dad to your future children someday. This list will be something that you can keep and reflect on as you meet guys in the future. This is important because unfortunately, when you first meet a guy, it's easy to get lost in the butterflies and puppy love causing you to lose track of your Mr. Right. However, this list can be used to ensure that you won't forget the man of God that you deserve.

Dear You,

Remember that love can be an incredible thing that changes your life, but be sure that you don't confuse it with emotions and temporary feelings. During this chapter of your life, I encourage you to build strong friendships instead of focusing on which guy you're going to date. A lot of things change throughout middle school and high school and into college. Who you are today isn't necessarily who you are going to be five years down the road. Likewise, who your Mr. Right is right now, may not be the man of God you will fall in love with later on down the road. This is because God is still working on him, just like He is working on you. Therefore, I encourage you during this time to be praying for the man you will someday marry. Pray for his walk with God, for his safety, for godly people to be placed in his life, and for God's love to surround him. Then, when you finally find him, rejoice but never forget that God isn't finished working in him and in you. Throughout it all, keep God as your focus and find your happiness in Him.

With Love,
Sarah

What qualities and characteristics do you want your Mr. Right to have?

Dear Lord,

I come before You today on behalf of my future husband. I pray that wherever he may be that You surround him with Your love. Please continue to work through his life so that he may become the man You created him to be. Help him to grow in strength, courage, and wisdom so that he may be the spiritual leader I need in my life. I pray for protection, both spiritual and physical, over his life. Lord, I also pray for Your guidance during this period of waiting so that I may become the woman my Mr. Right needs. In Your Son's name, I pray. Amen.

Ecclesiastes 3:11a (NIV)

Chapter 3

Life While Waiting in Your Tower

Ladies, get close to God before getting close
to anyone else. God without a man is still
God, but a man without God is nothing.

—Anonymous

*In a few months, I will turn 21 years old, and I still
haven't had my first kiss.*

*My name is Bethany, and for far too many years,
I thought I wasn't a full person because no man had
ever pursued me or shown interest in me. I began
to think there was something seriously wrong with*

me. As my closest friends in high school all began to find guys who would take them on dates, buy them flowers, and ask them to dances, I found myself having pity parties alone. I would mope in my sadness and my singleness. I thought it was like a plague, except it was only affecting me. I began to feel alone, but I would still pretend to be fine for everyone else's sake.

It wasn't until I came to college that I discovered how absolutely wrong I had been all along. I started seeking out God in every moment instead of trying to look cute so boys would notice me. I invested in my small group: a group of women my age from different walks of life who built me up and led me closer to Jesus.

One week, my small group had a panel of wise women come speak to us about relationships. When the woman who represented the single crowd spoke, one thing stuck with me: singleness is NOT the plague. You see, God calls us to embrace each season that we're in, and that's exactly what being single is: a season! Because I don't have a boyfriend, I am able to spend more time with Jesus and learn more about His character and how deeply He loves me. I am also learning how to love others in a similar fashion.

I would never lie to you and say that it has been

smooth sailing ever since I realized being single isn't the plague, but drawing nearer to Jesus in this season has been more beneficial than I can ever express. There is a God-shaped hole in our hearts, and if we try to fill that hole with anything but Jesus (such as a significant other), we will never truly be happy. God is the ultimate example of true love, so learn from the source of expertise first!

The other biggest realization that continues to provide hope in this season of "Waiting for Mr. Right" is gratitude. Gratitude can be one of your greatest sources of strength during times of waiting. Instead of moping, I have chosen to thank God for what He has given me during this season! I have some of the greatest friends in the world, and I can invest in them fully during this season because I'm not also trying to invest into a significant other. Rob Bell says, "This is why gratitude is so central to the life God made for us. Until we can center ourselves on what we do have, on what God has given us, on the life we do get to live, we'll constantly be looking for another life." Be thankful for what God has given you right now and live into the blessings and goodness He has for you!

We are surrounded by "love". Songs are written about it, movies portray it, and everyone seems to be talking about it. The belief that we need someone to "love" us and complete us is pushed on us, causing us, as young women, to desperately search for a Mr. Right who will show us love. However, what happens when we can't find him? It's easy to become discouraged and insecure when everyone around you begins to date while you don't. The Valentine's Days, the school dances, and all of the other times you're reminded that you are single lead you to think that you would be content if only you found your Mr. Right. Well, I'm here to tell you that you are not alone. Although during this time, you may want to quickly jump into a relationship, it's important to spend this period of waiting building your relationship with God.

Let's take a moment and imagine a typical day with your friends. How much of your conversation revolves around cute guys or your dream boyfriend? Now, throughout your conversations, how many times, if any, do you talk about where you are at in your relationship with God? It's easy to see where your focus is by taking a look at what your conversations and thoughts revolve around. Don't get me wrong, having someone to go on dates with and journey through life with is nice, but until you have a strong relationship with God, you will never be complete and always feel like something is missing.

We often forget that we were designed by God to be in a relationship with Him. Because of this, we have an imaginary hole in our hearts that can only be filled by God. Although many people try to fill this void with accomplishments, money, friends, possessions, and even the most perfect guy, the feeling of loneliness is still there. In fact, God is the ONLY one who can make us complete. That is why, while waiting for Mr. Right, you need to focus on growing closer to God while becoming the woman He created you to be. Likewise, not only are you still becoming a woman of God, but your Mr. Right is also still becoming the spiritual leader he needs to be. Your Mr. Right may not be your Mr. Right at this current time; he may still have a lot of growing to do. Therefore, what are you doing today to be the woman your Mr. Right is looking for?

Dear You,

I know it's hard. I know it can be difficult when your best friends all have plans with their boyfriends and you're stuck at home with ice cream and Netflix. I've been there. I get it. But take heart, my friend! The joy that God can bring you far exceeds the happiness that can come from a significant other. Finding joy in the small moments and embracing right where you are is such a beautiful thing.

What I know now is that comparison is a thief of joy, and no one is ever as happy as they look on social media. Trust me. Don't compare your beautiful, unique story with those of the people around you. God has made you unique and beautiful, and He wants to lead you into a life full of joy!

While you're waiting for "Mr. Right," spend time falling more in love with Jesus. He's the one who ultimately will fulfill you. You are fearfully and wonderfully made (Psalm 139:14), and no person can change that. Learn to love yourself exactly as you are, and in time, the Lord may lead you to someone who will ultimately help you look more like Jesus.

You are wonderful exactly as you are! Enjoy where you are now, and you can appreciate the next season when it's time.

With so much love for you,
Bethany Anne

What things have you used to try to fill the emptiness
in your heart?

While waiting for Mr. Right, what are you doing to build your relationship with God?

Dear Holy Father,

You are good in all of Your ways. Today I hand over to You each of the things that I have used to try to fill the emptiness in my heart. You are the one desire of my heart. Each day I will strive to live my life in a way that reflects the love You have shown me. In times of worry and uncertainty, I pray that I will find comfort in You. As I wait, my prayer is to become more and more like Your Proverbs Princess. Amen.

Proverbs 4:23 (NIV)

CHAPTER 4

When Mr. Right Becomes Mr. Wrong

The right relationship will never distract you
from God. It will bring you closer to Him.
—Anonymous

*"Forever and ever babe," he said with a smile that
made my heart melt. I believed and trusted in that
four-line phrase more than a lot of other things in
my life at the time. He was my friend before we had
dated. We "talked" a long while before dating for two
years, so I had a lot of time and emotion invested in
him. Needless to say, in high school I thought that he*

was my forever. However, my two-year relationship with my high school sweetheart had ended, and I was really distraught. It was a mutual break-up, and we had some pretty good reasons that kept us from being together. We were becoming different as we started heading in different directions. As I began my college career at a Christian college, it started to become clearer to me that the differences in the way we wanted to live our lives would be a constant problem. He agreed and wanted the same thing. After all the time, memories, and promises shared, one phone call to him from 127 miles away ended it all.

Time healed the raw emotion for me that I was feeling. Pure unspeakable joy came from the heartbreak. Following the break-up with my Mr. Wrong, I had a year full of so much love from family and friends. A lot of really good and exciting things started happening in my life once I began running in the right direction toward God and trusting His plan. I continued to live this very happy life full of joy, without really worrying about finding Mr. Right. I ended up creating a list of values and qualities that I was looking for in a future spouse. (This is something that I encourage everyone to do to ensure that they aren't settling for Mr. Wrong. Simply take a pen and write down what you are looking for in a man. There is even a place to do this in Chapter 2. Then, pray over those from time to time. Remind yourself, when God finally blesses you with a man who lines up with your list, that He is faithful.) Overall, I was finally healing and waiting. I found that I was fully content with life because of Jesus.

I wish I could say that it was all perfect from there but that wasn't the end. I was once again tempted into settling for Mr. Wrong, even with all of the progress I had made. I dated the guy that I was already over. I had honestly been over him, but there was still a tiny part of me that missed him, which is normal with any first love. You see, even when you are no longer with him, you are going to still have a special place in your heart for him. You'll always wonder how he is because at one point you truly cared about him and loved him. I think that it is so important to not get this feeling confused with actually missing him to the point where you get back together. I fell for him all over again and this time even faster than in high school. I figured that God wouldn't give something back that I had already once given up, but this wasn't the case. It was a test. On one hand, I would like to say that I passed the test with flying colors. However, then I wouldn't have learned the lesson of not settling and truly surrendering to God's will when it came to waiting for and finding Mr. Right.

As I was captivated by being in love again, I failed to realize how different we really were this time around. The differences between us ended up hurting my relationship with him in the future and ultimately had me running away from God. I pushed them aside and figured that they would change. Through revival services, a lot of thoughtful prayer and consideration, and one night of a rude awakening, I realized that what I had written in my journal back in December finally was answered. The question I wrote was, "Can my worldly desires be combined with what my heavenly Father desires?" The answer that I wanted so badly to be yes was simply no. It took a lot of time to understand why things had to end, but I think that we both learned to not settle.

Do not stray away from what God wants for your life. If He has placed a passion in your heart for a godly man, for someone to be on the same page as you when it comes to beliefs in alcohol or ways to live your daily life, do not push your standards and wants aside. You both should be getting what you want without hurting the other person. Neither one of us deserved to settle for someone who didn't fully agree with the other's views on very important areas *of life. Sometimes, when we decide to not settle, it ends with a really hard goodbye. However, in the end, you will find the person who is your Mr. Right and realize that God will not disappoint you.*

My Mr. Wrong had the way that he wanted to live and I had mine. In the end they didn't match. It wasn't fair to either one of us to keep the other one from the ways in which we wanted our lives to look. Yes, that realization is really heartbreaking after you spent so much time thinking that you would spend the rest of your life with a person. Still, like a friend once told me, "If you give something up, God will replace it." Personally, I strongly believe that most of the time it is replaced with something even better.

As you are growing up and entering the dating world, pray for God to send you Mr. Right and remember to never settle. We tend to settle when it comes to relationships because we feel insecure in our expectations, wants, and needs. We settle for less than what God has intended for us. Settling sometimes feels okay. However, when we allow God to give us God-sized dreams, then it will not work to settle because no matter how hard you want to change a person, you can't make him fit your list of expectations. It also isn't fair to the other person. Not settling sometimes hurts and always takes great courage, but we must trust that God has a plan.

If you are the person right now saying, "I am settling for Mr. Wrong," and you are running in the wrong direction, I encourage you to pray and seek for what the Lord wants you to do. If you haven't settled yet and you were going to, I pray that my story encourages you to not settle and keep waiting for Mr. Right. If you are the one that is dealing with the heartbreak of saying goodbye, my friend, joy is on its way.

Although we cannot travel back in time and tell ourselves everything we wish we would have known, we can share what we would tell our younger selves to help guide others.

Whether you are currently with a guy, considering talking to a guy, or in the future when you meet a guy, I want you to imagine his picture with a bunch of dots scattered across it. Each of these points represents a characteristic that he has. For example, one point could represent his passion for helping others while another is his love for sports or his desire to travel. Now, set that picture aside for a moment, and imagine the Mr. Right you previously described at the end of Chapter 2. Across your Mr. Right's image are also many dots that each symbolize a different quality you want him to display. Taking both pictures, place one on top of the other. The dots of the qualities that are shared by both will line up. Ideally, all of the dots should line up if the guy that you are interested in has all of the same qualities that you wanted your Mr. Right to have. As you look closely at both pictures, some of the dots are going to line up. Maybe both enjoy working with children, hiking, and reading. Therefore, since a couple of these dots line up, you begin to think that he must be your Mr. Right, so you continue in a relationship with him. As time goes on, red flags begin to appear as you realize more and more dots don't align. At this point, it's easy to make compromises, but I'm here to tell you NOT to ignore the red flags. You see, if something seems off or wrong about your relationship, that's probably because there is. It's important to realize that Mr. Wrong doesn't always appear to be the wrong guy at first. Oftentimes, he comes riding in on a white horse, saying all the right things, and promising to save you. However, each dot ignored and every compromise made leads to more heartache in the end. Your Mr. Right should be someone who leads you closer to God. He needs to accept you as you are; meanwhile, being with him should make you want to be the best possible version of yourself.

On the other hand, there could be a guy who loves God and is an all-around great guy but that doesn't automatically make him your Mr. Right. It's still important to make sure all the dots align. If you don't have the same interests and don't share the same vision for your life, then you are going to run into problems down the road.

Despite whether or not you think a guy is your Mr. Right, when you enter into a serious relationship, your two separate paths begin to become one. As you create memories together, make inside jokes, attend family gatherings, and learn each other's pasts, a bond starts to form, a bond that will only continue to grow. However, even if you enter into a relationship without the intention of marriage, this connection will still be created. This means that when you decide to end things, the bond will be broken, resulting in pain and hurt feelings. Now, the intention of this is not to discourage you from breaking up with someone. If you are with Mr. Wrong, then ending things, even if there will be pain, is the best option because it will save you from even more heartbreak in the future. However, I am encouraging you to be aware of whether or not you see a future with him before you enter into a relationship and then throughout the early days of your relationship.

Let's take a moment and illustrate this concept. I want you to picture two rose bushes that are planted next to each other at the beginning of spring. Throughout the summer, these two bushes will grow, and as they grow, they will become closer and closer. At some point, the stems and flowers of these two plants will begin to overlap and intertwine. Although they will still be two separate bushes, they will have become attached. Then, at the start of autumn, one of these bushes will be transplanted (the reason as to why is not important). However, this can't be done without parts having to be torn apart from the other plant, causing damage to each of the rose bushes. Although the rose bushes weren't planted with the intention of growing together and becoming attached, the fact that damage was caused in the end cannot be changed. You see, we like to believe that we can be in a romantic relationship with someone and not become attached, that we can somehow grow close to someone intimately but then bail out if things start to go wrong without getting hurt. Sadly, this usually just isn't true. Even if we don't realize it, as time goes on in a relationship, both people grow closer and closer, and their two lives become intertwined. This is why it is so important to figure out whether or not a guy you're interested in lines up with your criteria prior to the emotions and feelings of love. The longer you wait to decide whether or not he is the one, the closer you two will become and the more difficult it will be to walk away.

Therefore, regardless of whether you are currently in a relationship or just got out of one, know that you are not alone. Not only have countless girls gone through similar situations, also God is waiting for you to hand your broken pieces over to Him, so He can remind you of the princess that you were created to be.

To You,

You are loved. You are loved by the creator of all the earth and this is enough. His love is sufficient for you, and you do not need to seek any other type of love before you have sought His great love wholeheartedly. Continue to let Him take over your heart and seek a relationship with Him above all because after all, this relationship will be the only one that is everlasting.

A lot of things in your life right now are temporary, so seek the eternal love found in Jesus. When all else fades away, as it does a lot in this transitional period of life, you can have one constant. In the coming times, you will be tested; pray and seek so that you make the right decisions. Share the Good News and shine your light. Don't shy away just because the way you believe isn't the way that your classmates or boyfriend believes. Be a witness to them and let all of your life be an example.

When it comes to relationships, do not become tempted by allowing yourself to give your whole heart to someone else before you are ready. Pause. Ask yourself, "Do I see myself with this person for the rest of my life?" Just because it seems as though everyone else is running into someone else's arms, doesn't mean that it is your time. *Make sure you are being careful and considerate of your actions because they will affect your future forever. You might be young and in love now, but even as you grow older, your actions now will follow you for the rest of your life. Running into someone else's arms, if he is Mr. Wrong, will mean running away from God, so make sure above all else you guard your heart.*

Proverbs 4:20-23 (NIV): "My son (daughter), pay attention to what I say; turn your ear to my words. Do not let them out of your sight, keep them within your heart; for they are life to those who find them and health to one's body. Above all else, guard your heart, for everything you do flows from it."

Lace up your shoes and run in the right direction, my friend. And remember to take some moments along the run to catch your breath because everything will be okay if you just trust. No matter how hard the present moment gets, the future is full of joy and peace in Jesus.

Love,
Hannah

If you are currently talking to a guy, consider the following questions: (*If you are not, I encourage you to return to these questions in the future.*)

What are the top five characteristics that stand out about him?

What is he personally doing to grow closer to God himself, and how is he leading you towards God?

Does he hold the same qualities as your Mr. Right, or are you making compromises in your relationship?

What qualities are you not willing to compromise when it comes to finding Mr. Right?

What are some things you are going to do when meeting a guy to make sure he is the right one without getting caught up in emotions?

Dear Lord,

Today I hand over the pieces of my heart to You. Although I do not always understand, I trust in Your goodness and love. I thank You for loving me despite where I've been and what I've done. I pray that Your comfort and peace cover me during difficult times. I will look to You for guidance and walk in Your way. With love, I pray. Amen.

THEREFORE WHAT

God

J O I N E D

➤—together—➤

let no one

S·E·P·A·R·A·T·E

mark 10:9

Mark 10:9 (NIV)

CHAPTER 5

Life After the Happily Ever After

Marriage: The lifelong journey of
learning to love like Christ.
—Anonymous

*My mother has always said, "Everyone is going to
let you down, Mad: your friends, your family, your
husband, me. Everyone is going to let you down at
some point or another. Everyone ... except Jesus."*

*I can picture her smile while she says his name.
She is a wise woman. I suppose she knows from
experience. She knows because she has lived long*

enough to see everyone she loved and trusted let her down. And she knows because Jesus never did.

For me, coming into my marriage with Nate almost five years ago, this little piece of wisdom served me well. At times, I would lean too heavily on Nate and feel frustrated when he didn't live up to the standard I had in my head. Then, I would hear my mother's voice ringing clear in my ears and remember: the only perfect one is God. I don't feel frustrated with my husband after that; I feel thankful for him. He does his best for me and would never intentionally hurt me, but he is not God. And so I thank God for my husband, and ask God that as we walk this path with Him day after day, we would become more and more like Him. I have seen Him answering that prayer already.

Nowadays, it is popular to try and find "balance" in your life. Nate and I don't believe in balance; we believe in doing whatever God wants us to do. To tell this story, I first have to reveal our embarrassing-cutesy-couple-nickname for each other: Bunny. (You know like "honey bunny"?) I call him Bunny, and he calls me Bunny: we are the Bunnies. Now that you've stopped laughing, I can continue with the story. Early on in our marriage we developed a little saying, "Bunny second". You see, the thing I love best about my husband is that on his priority list I am not first; God is always first. When I say to my husband, "Bunny second," I am reminding him of two things. First, I want him to keep his head on straight and his eyes fixed on God. Second, I gently remind him of the covenant we made before God. He will say the same to me.

One mistake I have made in the past is to focus on fixing number two on my priorities list first. I will think about what it means to be a godly wife and how to love Nate like Jesus would and all that; however, it usually gets me nowhere. The best thing I have done for my marriage is to find a quiet corner and spend time with the One I love most. When I ask Nate-centered questions, I typically come up short. However, when I ask, "God, what do you want?" not only does my relationship with God get better, but everything in my life straightens out, including my marriage. Many are searching for peace, blindly believing that when they achieve the right balance in their life they will find it. This is wasted effort, for nothing brings peace like full surrender to the Prince of Peace. The one who seeks God will find Him.

We were created to be in relationship. Although I live, work, and hang out with people who are flawed and will let me down, I am not meant to go through this life alone. As a human being, I'm a mess-up too. So in my marriage and in my life, first I get alone with God, my all in all, and second, I go out into the world and give grace to my husband. Since that is what Christ did for me.

At some point in your life, you are going to come across a man who meets every criterion on your list for Mr. Right and will fall head over heels in love. You will go on adorable dates and finally get to use your Pinterest wedding board, but what happens after the honeymoon when real life begins? Have you ever noticed how almost every fairytale and chick flick ends after the lead woman finds Mr. Right and has her flawless wedding? Maybe there's a reason. Maybe married life isn't as perfect as everyone hopes. Maybe that's because many people enter into marriage without really knowing its purpose.

Marriage wasn't designed with the intention to complete us. Like mentioned earlier, no man and no marriage will fill that feeling of emptiness you have inside your heart. Only God is able to make you whole. In fact, the ultimate goal of marriage should be to help your spouse grow closer to God.

Picture marriage as a triangle with God at the top and the husband and wife at the lower corners. As each grows closer to God, they also grow closer to their spouse and vice-versa. When one begins to stumble, the other helps them back up. However, if one is not growing closer to God, the spouse has to make a decision: either grow closer to God and away from her spouse, or closer to her spouse and away from God. That is why it is extremely important that both you and your Mr. Right have strong faiths when you begin your relationship.

In terms of relationships, it's important for yours to be healthy. However, please know that healthy is not equivalent to perfect. A healthy, positive relationship is not one without flaws but instead, is one where two people see their flaws and problems and decide to work through them together. When something occurs to cause anger, rather than letting resentment build, the two decide to discuss what happened and work towards a solution. There must be trust and forgiveness in a healthy relationship. Most importantly, it means every day choosing to say, "I love you more than whatever we're going through," and "I am not giving up on us." You see, love is not a feeling but a choice. Initially, when you first meet your Mr. Right, there are going to be butterflies and the movie kind of love. Your first kiss is going to send your heart racing. You'll save each love letter and cute text he sends. You'll never forget the first time he held your hand or put his arm around you at the movies. You'll always cherish when you went on your first date, when he asked you to be his girlfriend, and when you met his friends and family. Unfortunately, as time goes on this feeling of infatuation begins to fade and real life replaces the fairytale romance. The little things he always does that are cute at first begin to become normal and even annoying at times. Worries and stresses of life can start to take the place of the carefree days when the world seemed to fade away every time you were together. It's easy during these times to think that love has ended and therefore so should your relationship. Yet, this is when, instead of giving up, you have the option to choose love. By choosing love, you are rising above the problem and as a result, showing Christ to your spouse.

Chick flicks and fairytales may seem appealing, but God has a greater plan for you. Despite where you may have been or currently are and regardless of whether you gave your heart to the wrong guy or are struggling with being single, God has been and always will be there waiting for you to place your heart in His hands. Leave your focus on Him and on becoming the Proverbs Princess you were created to be. That way, when Mr. Right comes your way, you will be ready to enter into the journey of life together.

Dear You,

Please eat more vegetables.

Also, don't be afraid of being wrong. Open up to those around you, but don't be proud. Listen and be ready to learn. Some of your failures will end up being the best lessons. Learning can be hard and life can hurt. However, growing is special and important, and people won't remember the little details that keep you up at night.

Most importantly, listen to God, and do what He says. Sometimes this is boring, and sometimes it means waiting. Other times, you will go on wild adventures like marrying your husband or moving across the country with him (twice). God will guide you through each season in its time. And don't worry about money. It's not important. Your God owns the cattle on a thousand hills. See the lilies grow? And the birds that neither sow nor reap nor gather into barns? Aren't they taken care of? And aren't you more important than they? God will take care of you (Matthew 6). Remain steadfast. Remember all of the times He didn't let you down. Meditate on them, and on His Word. Through it all, be thankful.

Love,
Mad

Consider any of the marriages that people in your life have; in what ways is God involved in their marriage? How do they help each other grow closer to God and stay accountable? What qualities have you seen lived out that you one day want to incorporate into your marriage?

What qualities do you believe a healthy relationship should have?

What are some things that couples can do to put God first?

How can you personally continue to grow in your relationship with God once you are married?

Dear Heavenly Father,

Although I may not be married now, I pray that you become present in my life and in every relationship that I may have, now and in the future. I pray that my future marriage will bring glory to Your name as it shines as an example of our relationship as Christians with You. I ask that You will be with me when I one day walk down the aisle to marry a man after Your heart. I ask that You will bless our marriage as we build our foundation in You. You are the source of my joy and strength, and I will praise You throughout every moment of my life. Thank You for Your grace and endless love. In your holy name, I pray. Amen.

Dear Lord,

All of Your ways are good, even when they don't always make sense to us. We pray that regardless of what chapter of our lives we may be in, our trust is placed in You. Each day, we strive to reflect more of Your selfless love as we grow to know You more. Let us be a light in our homes, schools, and wherever else we may go. With courage and strength, we stand up for what is right and help those around us. We are placing all the broken pieces of our hearts in Your hands as we walk in the forgiveness and healing that You provide. With all that we are and with all that we do, we praise Your name and give thanks for every blessing You have placed in our lives.

With Love,
Your Proverbs Princesses

Made in the USA
Middletown, DE
03 January 2017